The Library of
Future Weather and Climate

Droughts
of the Future

Paul Stein

The Rosen Publishing Group, Inc.
New York

Published in 2001 by The Rosen Publishing Group, Inc.
29 East 21st Street, New York, NY 10010

Copyright © 2001 by The Rosen Publishing Group, Inc.

First Edition

Library of Congress Cataloging-in-Publication Data
Stein, Paul, 1968–
Droughts of the future / Paul Stein. — 1st ed.
p. cm. — (The library of future weather and climate)
Includes bibliographical references and index.
ISBN 0-8239-3411-X (lib. bdg.)
1. Droughts—Juvenile literature. 2. Climatic changes—Environmental aspects—Juvenile literature. [1. Droughts. 2. Climatic changes.] I. Title.
QC929.25 .S74 2001
551.57'73—dc21

00-012138

All temperatures in this book are in degrees Fahrenheit, except where specifically noted. To convert to degrees Celsius, or centigrade, use the following formula:

Celsius temperature = (5 ÷ 9) x (the temperature in Fahrenheit - 32)

Manufactured in the United States of America

Contents

Introduction

We are watery people living on a watery planet. Water is one of the most important molecules of our world because it supports life. From oceans to lakes to ponds and streams, water covers 80 percent of the earth's surface. Of all the water that exists on our planet, 97 percent is contained in the oceans. Around 2 percent of the earth's water is locked up in the vast ice sheets that cap the North and South Poles, or in glaciers that drape the sides of mountains. Less than 1 percent is freshwater, found in rivers, streams, lakes, and ponds.

Despite this relative scarcity of drinkable freshwater, most of us give little thought to our water supply. Weather systems spin and sweep across the globe at regular intervals, delivering needed rain and snow to our reservoirs and rivers. Turn on the tap in the kitchen sink, and freshwater comes pouring out. We generally don't need to think about it.

Every once in a while, however, the rain and snow dwindle. Weather patterns shift and carry storm systems away from us. When this happens for an extended period of time and the water supply falls well below normal, the land is said to be in a state of drought. The effects of a drought can range from dried-up suburban lawns to devastating famine affecting millions of people. Drought sucks water from the earth, and in so doing threatens life's fragile existence. Even so, droughts are naturally occurring phenomena related to events in the earth's atmosphere. In the decades to come, droughts will continue to parch different parts of the world from time to time just as they have done throughout history.

Consider the Mayan civilization, for example, which flourished in parts of modern-day Mexico, Guatemala, and Belize more than a thousand years ago. Over a period of hundreds of years, starting around AD 250, the Mayans grew into an advanced civilization that developed a complex system of agriculture and made discoveries in mathematics and astronomy. At its height, the Mayan civilization included over forty cities with a total population of two million. But sometime around AD 800, the Mayan civilization abruptly collapsed. A recent theory relates the cause of the collapse to a devastating drought that gripped the Central American region. During this time, the climate was the driest in 7,000 years. Crop failures may have led

Drought led to the dust bowl in the U.S. Midwest during the 1930s, disrupting the lives of millions of farmers and their families.

to competition for food and an increasing strain on society. This strain may have contributed to the outbreak of warfare and the irreversible and rapid decline of the Mayan civilization.

Fast forward to the central United States in the 1930s, the time of the "dust bowl." Year after year of scant rainfall and intense heat, along with poor farming and grazing practices, turned parts of the southern Plains states into a wasteland. Some areas were reduced to little more than a desert landscape. Great cloudy walls of dust over a thousand feet high engulfed everything in their path as they blew across the barren fields. Hundreds of millions of tons of topsoil were removed from the land, with some of the dust falling from the sky as far away as Washington, DC. The drought led to the greatest migration in American history as millions of farmers and their families left to find work elsewhere.

And more recently, across sub-Saharan Africa from the late 1960s to the present day, drought has wrought suffering on a massive scale. This part of Africa, lying between the barren Sahara Desert to the north and the wet, tropical forests of central Africa to the south, is a fragile zone of transition in the African climate. Rainfall comes in cycles, sometimes plentiful, sometimes scarce. From Senegal and Mauritania in the west, to Sudan, Ethiopia, and Somalia in the east, year after year of below-normal rainfall has combined with land misuse to produce a devastating famine. Well over a hundred thousand people have died. As the ground has dried out, the Sahara Desert has expanded southward, taking over the landscape in a process known as desertification.

And what about the future? The earth's recent warming trend may lead to changes in the way water is cycled between the land, its lakes and oceans, and the sky. Scientists think this change in world climate, known as global warming, has been caused by the release of certain gases into the earth's atmosphere. Most important among these gases is carbon dioxide, which is produced through the burning of fossil fuels such as coal, natural gas, and oil. These fuels supply most of our energy needs, from electric power plants to automobile engines. As we consume more energy and pump more of these gases into the sky, many experts think that the global warming trend will continue through the twenty-first century. A warming planet means changes in the processes that control weather, including the natural cycle of drought.

This book tells the story of droughts, how they develop and how they are related to the natural cycle of water on our planet. It examines the phenomenon of global warming and the ways in which global warming might have an effect on droughts of the future.

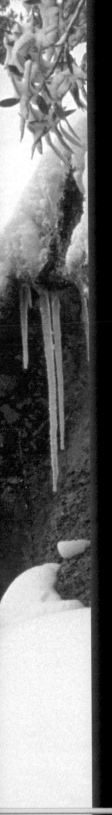

1 The Water Cycle

In order to understand the nature of droughts, we first need to think about water and how it behaves both on land and in the sky. The behavior of water involves the blowing of the wind, the relentless tug of gravity, and the dance of countless billions of tiny molecules. It involves the widest oceans and the smallest streams. And, of course, it involves all life on earth, including our own bodies, two-thirds of which are water.

Water is an extraordinary substance. It's the only molecule to exist in three different forms, or phases, in the normal range of the earth's temperature. These phases include ice, the solid phase of water; liquid, which we're most familiar with; and water vapor, the invisible, gaseous phase of water. The fact that water can exist in three different phases permits the continuous cycling

Water is the only compound on the earth that exists in three different phases—liquid, solid, and gas—within the normal range of the planet's temperature.

of water from the sky to the earth, with detours into plants and animals and our own bodies. This cycle of water is known as the hydrologic cycle, from the Greek word "hydro," meaning water.

Central to the hydrologic cycle are two processes in which water changes from one phase to another. The first is the process of evaporation, in which water changes from liquid form to gaseous water vapor. When water exists in a liquid state, water molecules are packed together loosely. Each individual molecule is constantly jostling around, hitting up against other water molecules, and bouncing off in random directions. On the surface of the water, where it meets the air, a molecule sometimes gains enough energy from this jostling to bounce into the air. Water molecules that jump free into the air like this are said to evaporate. They become individual water vapor molecules, too small to be seen with the unaided eye, that float away on air currents. The drying of puddles after rain and the vanishing of clouds from the sky are both examples of the process of evaporation.

The other important process in which water changes phase is called condensation, and it is the opposite of evaporation. It occurs when individual, freely floating water vapor molecules turn back into liquid water. Typically, this happens when the water vapor molecules collide with liquid water or with a solid object and stick to it. For example, water vapor molecules may bump into one another in the air and condense into a tiny liquid cloud droplet. Or they may collide with the surface of a lake or an ocean. Morning dew on grass forms by the process of condensation, as do water drops on a cold can of soda on a summer afternoon.

Water droplets form on leaves as a result of condensation from the air on humid mornings.

Yet another process, called sublimation, occurs when frozen water changes directly into water vapor without first melting. But the most important and common processes are evaporation and condensation, which occur simultaneously and continuously on the earth's surface and in its atmosphere. Water molecules are always bouncing free and evaporating from the surface of lakes and oceans, or from cloud droplets. At the same time, water vapor molecules in the air are always colliding with one another, or with water on the earth's surface, and condensing. The important thing to consider is which process, condensation or evaporation, is occurring faster.

The rates of evaporation and condensation depend in large part on temperature and on the amount of water vapor in the air. Generally speaking, the higher the temperature, the more water molecules will evaporate. This is because of the relationship between temperature and molecular motion. At a higher temperature, liquid water molecules move around faster and are more likely to break free from one another. Similarly, a lower temperature favors condensation over evaporation, since molecules move more slowly on average and can more easily stick to one another. But another important factor is the humidity of the air. Humidity is a term used to describe the amount of water vapor molecules in the atmosphere. With a higher humidity, more collisions occur among water vapor molecules and the rate of condensation increases. The fewer water vapor molecules there are, the less frequently they will collide and condense into liquid water.

Armed with a basic knowledge of the processes of evaporation and condensation, therefore, we follow the hydrologic cycle, the grand circulation of water between the earth's surface and its atmosphere. We start with runoff, the gravity-driven process in which water flows from higher elevations to lower elevations and eventually into the oceans. Runoff comes from precipitation, which is just a scientific term for rain, snow, and anything else watery that forms inside clouds and falls to the ground. A soaking rainstorm runs off in rivulets and streams down the street and into the sewer, or directly into larger streams and rivers. Or the rainwater just soaks into the ground, some of it percolating down into large underground reservoirs, and some drawn upward into plants. During colder weather, snow collects on the ground and eventually melts, running off or soaking into the soil.

Precipitation and runoff are the most obvious parts of the hydrologic cycle. The next step is mostly invisible. This is the process of evaporation, liquid water's vanishing act. Before the runoff from rain or melting snow ever gets to the oceans, some of it has evaporated back into the sky as water vapor. Another way that water vapor is released back into the air from the earth's surface is through a process called transpiration. In this process, plants and trees give off some of their stored water through tiny pores on the undersides of their leaves.

The greatest source of water vapor, however, is the ocean. Scientists estimate that 85 percent of the water vapor in the atmosphere comes from evaporation from the ocean surface. Carried aloft by air currents, water vapor molecules can rise miles into the sky. They can be blown across oceans and continents, many miles from their point of origin. In fact, the air you breathe now may contain water vapor molecules from a distant sea on the other side of the world.

An overabundance of runoff can result from fast-melting snow or ice, or from heavy rainfall.

The next part of the hydrologic cycle involves the formation of clouds in the sky. Clouds form from processes that occur in rising air. When air rises, it moves into regions of lower air pressure because there are less molecules weighing down from above. Moving into lower pressure, the air is able to expand and become less dense. Air molecules (including water vapor) therefore move around more slowly on average, and the air cools. The colder the air gets, the more frequently molecules will collide, stick together, and condense. When the rate of condensation exceeds the rate of evaporation, a cloud forms.

There are many other details in the process of cloud formation, but for our purposes here we will merely consider clouds growing in the sky. The more water vapor that's available, and the higher the air rises, the larger the clouds become. Most clouds contain both water droplets and ice crystals. Often, clouds grow only to a certain size before evaporating and releasing their water back into the atmosphere in the form of water vapor. However, if the cloud particles are able to grow large enough, the force of gravity takes over and they fall to the ground as snow or rain.

We return to where we started, with precipitation falling from the sky, running off into streams and rivers, and soaking into the ground. Across the earth, the total amount of water in the hydrologic cycle remains nearly the same. But the relative importance of each part of the cycle varies in different regions and at different times. For instance, precipitation and runoff rarely occur in deserts but are a continual event in tropical rain forests. Sometimes there is an abundance of water, too much too fast, from a heavy rain or a large amount of fast-melting snow. At other times, however, rain falls infrequently, and evaporation becomes dominant, leading to drought. In the next chapter, we discuss how droughts occur and the weather patterns that spawn them.

2 Droughts

Lacking the violence of a tornado or the force of a flood, drought is a disaster in disguise. It occurs gradually, squeezing water from the land over months. But the effects can be as costly as the most vicious storm.

Consider, for example, the drought that parched much of the United States in the summer of 1988. The dry conditions began as early as April across the northern Plains and Midwest. Week after week of below-average rainfall slowly took its toll on the land. By the middle of summer, many parts of the central and western United States had received less than half of their normal precipitation. June was especially dry. Minneapolis, Minnesota, recorded only 0.22 inches of rain that month, just 5 percent of normal rainfall. To the north, St. Cloud, Minnesota, received a mere 1 percent of normal rainfall.

Droughts can ravage farmland, especially when accompanied by a summer heat wave.

By mid July, 45 percent of the lower forty-eight states were suffering severe drought conditions. Adding to the misery, the summer of 1988 was the hottest on record in many locations. From Montana and Wyoming in the west to Michigan in the east, temperatures routinely soared into the 90s and 100s. Dozens of weather stations recorded new high temperature records, including Sioux Falls, South Dakota, with a desertlike 110°F.

It seemed as though the rain refused to fall. Crops withered in the fields, with corn and soybean farmers hit especially hard. From June through August, Kansas City, Missouri, had just 3.27 inches of rain, a small fraction of the nearly 11 inches that normally fall in this period. For the country as a whole, it was the driest summer in over fifty years. To the west, in Yellowstone National Park in Wyoming, forest fires fueled by dry trees burned over 800,000 acres of land. To the east, the Mississippi River shrank to a shadow of its former size, with numerous sandbars blocking barge traffic over long stretches. Across the nation as a whole, the damage estimate amounted to $40 billion, much of it from crop losses and energy costs. By comparison, Hurricane

Andrew, the most damaging hurricane ever to strike the United States, caused $27 billion in damage as it blasted across southern Florida in August 1992.

The drought itself was caused by a stubborn weather event known to meteorologists as a "blocking pattern." This kind of weather pattern occurs when a large mass of air with relatively high air pressure and high temperature sits over the same region for a long period of time. The air mass can be

Woodland areas, where trees dry out during a drought, become especially susceptible to forest fires.

many hundreds of miles wide. Storm systems following jet stream winds from the west are forced around the blocking area of high pressure. Within the air mass, air currents slowly descend from high altitudes to low altitudes. Since clouds grow in rising air, this sinking motion prevents clouds from becoming large enough to produce rain. Blocking patterns are often linked by meteorologists to changes in ocean water temperatures thousands of miles away. A large area of warmer than normal or cooler than normal ocean water can warm and cool the air above it, leading to changes in weather patterns. Sometimes these changes include the formation of a persistent, drought-causing blocking pattern.

The most notorious examples of these kinds of ocean temperature antics are the phenomena of El Niño and La Niña. El Niño occurs when water temperatures rise above normal in the tropical eastern Pacific. La Niña, just the opposite, happens when water temperatures fall below normal in the same area. A change in ocean water temperature causes a change in the temperature of the air above it. It also affects the humidity of the air, since temperature helps determine the rate of evaporation. For example, El Niño–warmed ocean water typically raises the temperature of the air over the tropical eastern Pacific. It also adds water vapor to the air. When these kinds of changes happen over a large area, weather patterns can shift from their normal patterns. And changing weather patterns in one part of the world often have a ripple effect around the planet.

The result is that strong El Niño and La Niña events have come to be associated with unusually wet and dry weather in various parts of the world. El Niño is known to contribute to drought conditions over Southeast Asia and northern Australia, as well as parts of southern Africa. When La Niña occurs, on the other hand, dry weather becomes more likely across the southern United States and in parts of northern South America, near the Pacific coast. Scientists are becoming better

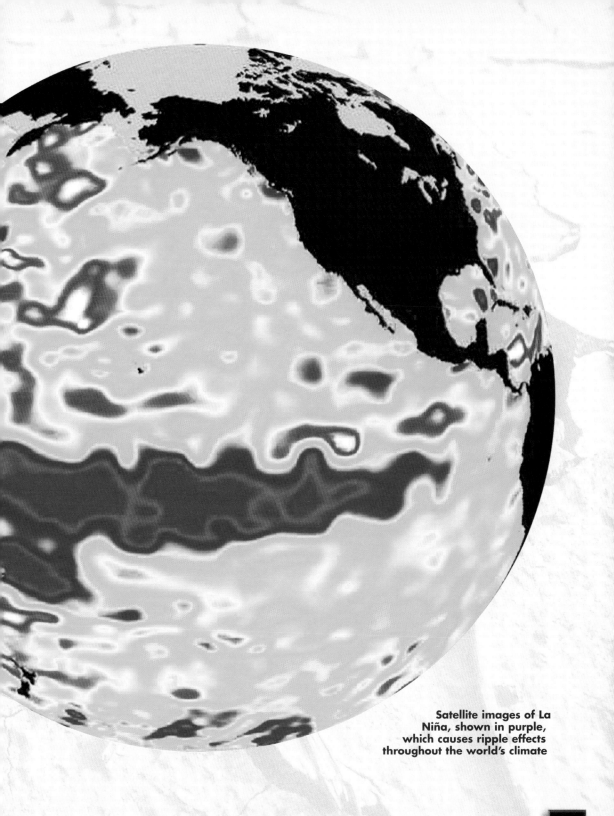

Satellite images of La Niña, shown in purple, which causes ripple effects throughout the world's climate

able to predict these changes in the oceans in advance, but have yet to unravel all the details associated with this complex interaction between oceans and atmosphere.

No matter what the cause, there are three different ways to define drought. In a meteorological drought, the most important factor is the lack of precipitation. In an agricultural drought, the focus is on crops, their water needs during different growing stages, and the amount of moisture in the soil. Hydrologic drought is based upon the amount of water flowing through rivers and streams compared to normal conditions. Meteorological, agricultural, and hydrologic drought are just three different ways of looking at the same natural phenomena.

Drought can be one of the most costly kinds of natural disaster. The drought of 1988 was an extreme example of what happens when rainfall dwindles for an extended period of time. But there's more to a drought than just a lack of rain. Drought must be considered in relation to other natural factors, all of which are part of the hydrologic cycle.

To start with, the amount of precipitation considered average for a particular region is important. For example, during the summer months of June, July, and August, Sacramento, California, normally receives a mere 0.2 inches of rain. Miami, Florida, on the other hand, typically gets well over twenty inches during the same period. So Miami would most certainly be in a severe drought if it received only 0.2 inches of rain during the summer. But the same amount in Sacramento would be business as usual. Drought results not from a low amount of rainfall, but a low amount of rainfall relative to what's average for the location.

Evaporation and transpiration must also be considered when thinking about drought. When talking about these two processes together, scientists use the term "evapotranspiration." Remember, evaporation is the process by which liquid water changes into gaseous water vapor. Transpiration is the process by which plants release liquid water into the air through pores on the undersides of their leaves. Evapotranspiration, then, removes water from the ground and adds it to the atmosphere. While this is happening, the water lost by the ground is replaced by precipitation falling from the sky. Usually the processes of precipitation and evapotranspiration balance each other. This natural balance determines the supply of water in a given area. However, when evapotranspiration is greater than precipitation, more water evaporates into the atmosphere than is absorbed by the ground from precipitation. If this imbalance in the hydrologic cycle persists for weeks or months, a drought sets in.

The amount of evapotranspiration depends mainly on weather conditions—temperature, wind, sunshine, and humidity. The higher the

Transpiration is the process by which plants release water into the atmosphere.

A farmer in Oklahoma examines a ravaged cornfield in 1988, when severe drought hit the Midwest.

temperature, the higher the rate of evaporation. Gusty winds, low humidity, and bright sunshine also increase the amount of water vapor leaving the ground. This is one of the reasons that drought is often most severe during the summer months, when the air is at its hottest and sunshine at its brightest.

Plants and drought are related in another way. As precipitation drops well below average and drought takes hold of the landscape, plants begin to suffer from lack of water. Small plants and crops are the first to die, then larger plants and trees may follow if drought conditions become severe enough. With fewer plants releasing water into the air through the process of transpiration, the humidity levels drop and drought conditions worsen. As plants die, more and more sunlight is able to reach the ground and dry it out. This effect is particularly important where crops cover large tracts of land and are an important source of water vapor in the air. With less water vapor in the air, clouds form less readily and rainfall becomes even scarcer.

Another factor in droughts is the way in which humans use the land. A drought may become more severe if good agricultural and grazing practices are not followed. For example, the dust bowl of the 1930s in the Plains states was made worse by unwise land use. Farmers removed trees to expand their fields, and in so doing took away a natural barrier to the wind. Wind speeds increased, quickly drying out the ground and blowing away topsoil in great storms of dust. Likewise, in some African nations in the last half of the twentieth century, local herders allowed cattle and goats to overgraze the land, stripping and killing the natural vegetation over wide areas. This quickened the pace of drought and allowed the expansion of the Sahara Desert southward into areas that once were grassland.

In summary, drought evolves slowly over time, taking weeks and even months to set in. Plants, animals, and humans all play a role in determining how severe a drought may become. But the most important cause of a drought is the weather. Drought is an event that occurs when the amount of water leaving the ground through evapotranspiration is much greater than the amount entering the ground from precipitation. The typical rate of evapotranspiration and precipitation depends on the average weather conditions, including temperature, wind, and humidity. But what if the average weather conditions were to change? What effect would a changing climate have on drought? Before we answer this question, we first must look at how and why the earth's climate may be changing through the twenty-first century.

3 Our Warming Planet

Residents of Texas are no strangers to dry, hot weather. From Lubbock in the west to Dallas in the north to San Antonio in the south, triple-digit temperatures are commonplace during the summer months. The summer of 2000, however, was hot even by Texas standards. And oddly enough, the peak of the heat came in early September, a time when the sweltering summer air should be starting to cool down. But not that September, when the temperature in Dallas shot over 100°F a record seven times. The hottest day of all was September 4, when the mercury soared to 111°F—an all-time record for the month. Other cities around Texas

A dry pond in Haslet, Texas, in August 2000, following fifty-seven consecutive days without measurable precipitation, most of them during the height of a blistering summer.

recorded equally incredible temperatures that day, including 112°F in College Station and 109°F in Houston.

Some of these temperatures shattered the old records by as much as ten degrees. And with the heat came the drought. By the third week of September, Dallas had recorded a record eighty-four consecutive days with no measurable rainfall.

The dry, hot, late summer weather in Texas in the year 2000 was certainly remarkable. But as we've seen, heat waves and droughts are to be expected as a normal part of our changing weather. Even so, it is possible that the record Texas heat was a small part of a much larger trend. In recent years, scientists have recorded a warming of the entire planet—not in all locations at the same time, but on average across the globe. For example, 1999 was the twenty-first consecutive year in which the global mean temperature was above the long-term average. The ten warmest years in recorded history, dating back nearly a century and a half, all occurred since the early 1980s. The 1990s were the warmest decade in recorded history, with 1998 being the warmest year of all. And by reconstructing global temperature trends over the last thousand years, researchers were able to state that in all likelihood, the 1990s were the warmest decade of the millennium.

Meanwhile, at an observatory near the summit of the Mauna Kea volcano on the big island of Hawaii, scientists have been measuring atmospheric carbon dioxide levels for over four decades. The concentration of CO_2 as measured at Mauna Kea

Scientists near the Mauna Kea volcano in Hawaii, shown here, have observed a steady increase in carbon dioxide in the earth's atmosphere.

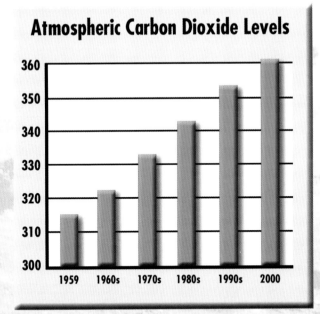

Atmospheric Carbon Dioxide Levels

Scientists theorize that rising levels of CO_2 and other gases are contributing to global warming on Earth.

has shown a persistent and disturbing upward trend. In 1959, the first year of measurements, scientists recorded a concentration of 315 parts per million, or ppm for short. In other words, out of every million air molecules, an average of 315 were molecules of carbon dioxide. From 315 ppm in 1959, the concentration of carbon dioxide rose above 320 ppm in the 1960s, over 330 ppm in the 1970s, past 340 ppm in the 1980s, and up to 360 ppm at the turn of the century. And the numbers continue to increase.

Scientists think there is a relationship between rising levels of carbon dioxide and other kinds of gases, and rising temperatures. What makes carbon dioxide so special? Carbon dioxide, amounting to only 0.036 percent of air on average, is an especially efficient absorber of a kind of energy known as radiation. Radiation consists of invisible electromagnetic waves traveling at the speed of light. All objects emit radiation. Trees emit radiation, as do rocks, houses, and people. The Sun obviously emits radiation, but so does the earth and the earth's atmosphere. And not only does everything

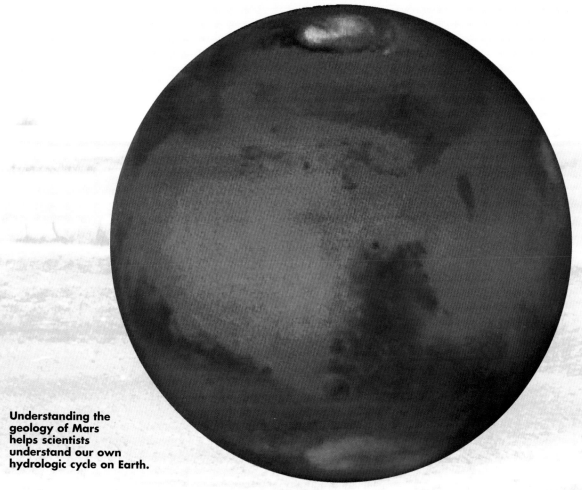

Understanding the geology of Mars helps scientists understand our own hydrologic cycle on Earth.

send out radiation, but every-thing also absorbs incoming radiation.

Both incoming and outgoing radiation contribute to the total energy, and therefore the temperature, of an object. If the object gives off more radiation than it receives, it cools. If an object absorbs more radiation than it gives off, it warms. The temperature of the surface of the earth, for example, depends on a balance of incoming radiation from the Sun, called solar radiation, and outgoing radiation from the surface of the earth, called terrestrial radiation.

A scientist adjusts an ultraviolet light monitor at McMurdo Station at the South Pole. Part of the U.S. Antarctic Program, the equipment gauges levels of radiation hitting the southern ice cap.

But there is also a continuous transfer of radiation from the ground to the atmosphere, and from the atmosphere to the ground. This exchange of radiation is the source of the now-famous greenhouse effect. It's a natural process, without which life as we know it could not exist on earth. The greenhouse effect is the warming effect the atmosphere has on our planet. It arises from the constant, invisible exchange of radiation up and down between the air and the earth. The earth emits terrestrial radiation upward, some of which is absorbed by the atmosphere. As this outgoing radiation is absorbed, energy is added to the air molecules. These molecules are already continuously radiating energy of their own, and the more terrestrial radiation they absorb, the more radiation they emit. Some of this radiation is emitted downward, where it is absorbed by the earth, causing the earth to warm. Without the greenhouse effect, the average temperature of our planet would be well below freezing. With the greenhouse effect, our average temperature is near 60°F.

This is where carbon dioxide comes in. Carbon dioxide acts as a kind of volume control on the greenhouse effect. The higher the amounts of CO_2 in the atmosphere, the more outgoing terrestrial radiation is absorbed. As the atmosphere absorbs more of this radiation, it gains energy and emits more radiation toward the ground, which warms even more as a result. Because of its contribution to the greenhouse effect, carbon dioxide is called a greenhouse gas. Other greenhouse gases include methane, nitrous oxide, ozone, and chlorofluorocarbons. Scientists think that the increasing amount of these greenhouse gases in the atmosphere, especially carbon dioxide, is at least partially responsible for the rising temperatures observed all around the planet.

Why are the levels of greenhouse gases increasing? One of the ways that scientists have answered this question is by drilling 10,000 feet down through the ice on Antarctica and Greenland. Ice contains a remarkable record of the earth's climate over thousands of years. As layers of snow fall year after year, each layer compacts under higher layers and eventually hardens into ice. Trapped within the ice are air bubbles—tiny records of the gaseous composition of the air

Coal, among other fossil fuels, is extracted from the earth and used to create energy for industry an consumers. However, burning fossil fuels also releases huge amounts of CO_2 into the air.

at the time a particular layer formed. Scientists drill into the ice to extract long tubular samples, called ice cores. They then examine the trapped bubbles in the ice cores to see how much CO_2 they contain. The deeper into the ice they drill, the further back in time they can look. In fact, ice cores from Antarctica have given scientists a glimpse of the earth's climate 200,000 years ago.

Using ice core data, scientists have been able to determine that the steadily increasing trend in atmospheric CO_2 now being recorded on Mauna Loa actually began sometime between the late eighteenth century and early nineteenth century. This was the period of time known as the Industrial Revolution. During the Industrial Revolution, people discovered that coal could be burned as a source of energy. Coal was mined from the ground in greater and greater volume, first in England, then in other parts of western Europe, then in the United States. Coal and steam provided the energy that ran factories. The discoveries of oil and natural gas soon followed. Then came trains, automobiles, trucks, and planes. Today, most of us use electricity generated in power plants that burn fossil fuels for energy.

So how do fossil fuels relate to the increase in carbon dioxide? Fossil fuels are so named because they are created from the ancient remains of animals and plants that have been compressed deep underground. Plants, like all organic matter, are made from carbon. Over millions of years of pressure far beneath the surface of the earth, the carbon inside these fossilized plants transformed itself into natural gas, oil, and coal. By extracting these fossil fuels from the ground and burning them for energy, we release carbon dioxide into the atmosphere.

By examining ice cores, scientists can re-create the presence of carbon dioxide in our atmosphere over time. Before the Industrial Revolution, the concentration of atmospheric CO_2 was fairly steady at around 280 ppm. Since the Industrial Revolution, as humans have released greater and greater amounts of carbon dioxide into the atmosphere through the burning of fossil fuels, the level of CO_2 has increased 30 percent. In fact, scientists now think that the current amount of CO_2 in the atmosphere is the highest amount in the last 420,000 years.

What effect has this had on the average temperature of our planet? The average global temperature at the end of the twentieth century was about 1°F higher than at the beginning of the century. While one degree seems small, it's significant considering that the planet has warmed by only 5° to 9°F since the last ice age, 18,000 to 20,000 years ago. What's more, the rate of temperature rise seems to be accelerating. This trend of rising temperatures is referred to as global warming.

Each year we inject seven billion metric tons of carbon dioxide into the atmosphere. At the current rate of increase, carbon dioxide levels will double before the end of the twenty-first century. Scientists think that largely because of this increase in carbon dioxide, the average temperature of the earth will rise anywhere from 3° to almost 11°F. Some predict that this will result in the fastest rate of climate change in the last 10,000 years.

It probably comes as no surprise that global warming may result in more frequent and severe droughts. Droughts are naturally linked to hot weather, though drought conditions can occur in any season. In the next chapter, we examine how global warming and changing climate may dry out parts of our planet in the decades to come, and what the consequences of future droughts may be.

4 Droughts of the Future

The largest area of sand dunes anywhere in North or South America is not located in a desert. It is not along the sandy beaches of any coastline. It is in the Great Plains of the United States, in the western part of the state of Nebraska to be exact. Here, in a region better known for fields of corn and wheat, lies an area of sand dunes covering nearly 20,000 square miles. That's fifteen times the size of the state of Rhode Island. Known as the Nebraska Sand Hills, the dunes are as long as ten miles, and as high as 300 feet. Unlike the typical Saharan Desert sand dune, however, these sand dunes are covered with a layer of wild grass. Numerous shallow lakes dot the landscape in between the dunes. Antelope and deer roam the hills, while a variety of birds

Natural formations, such as Colorado's Great Sand Dunes National Monument, which borders the Rocky Mountains, give us valuable clues as to how climate has changed over thousands of years.

and ducks live on the lakes. The origin of these dunes tells us a lot about changing climate and drought.

Currently, this part of North America gets about twenty inches of rain per year. That's enough to grow grass and shrubs, which prevent the sand dunes from moving with the blowing wind. But it hasn't always been this way. As recently as 1,500 years ago, scientists think the Nebraska Sand Hills were "active," meaning that they looked and behaved a lot like sand dunes found in a desert. They slowly moved across the landscape and grew in height as sand blew from one side of the dune to the other. Thousands of years ago, modern-day Nebraska was much drier than it is today. Rainfall probably amounted to less than ten inches. And strong winds helped dry things out even more.

The dry and windy weather combined to create a perfect climate for the formation of sand dunes.

The Nebraska Sand Hills clearly show that the climate of North America, like the climate everywhere else on the planet, naturally changes with time. It's not so obvious in the course of a lifetime, but over hundreds or thousands of years, the climate of a region can change drastically. A dry climate with sand dunes can turn into a wetter climate with grassland and lakes. And the opposite can happen, too. Global warming poses the possibility of changing climate and changing landscapes in the future. Part of this change may occur as droughts become more severe and last longer in certain regions of the world.

Global warming is linked to drought through the process of evaporation. Recall that evaporation occurs as liquid water changes into invisible, gaseous water vapor. On the molecular level, a jostling water molecule gains enough energy to break its liquid bonds and fly off into the air. The rate at which this occurs depends largely on temperature. The warmer the air and water, the faster the molecules move around and the more likely they are to break free from one another and evaporate. Water will leave the soil faster, causing the land to dry out more quickly. In a warmer world, therefore, drought may set in earlier and last longer than it does today.

Strangely enough, the same process may lead to more frequent and severe floods. The higher the rate of evaporation, the more water vapor is added to the atmosphere. Clouds and storms can become wetter and produce heavier precipitation in a shorter period of time. It makes sense, since the hydrologic cycle is just that—a cycle, or circular process. Turn up the volume on one part of the process, evaporation, and you increase the volume on another part of the process, precipitation.

This poses a question. If evaporation raises the atmosphere's humidity and spawns heavier rainstorms, wouldn't that tend to lessen the effects of drought, or even prevent them? Even though the ground loses moisture faster to the air, wouldn't precipitation just be that much heavier? The answer to this puzzle lies in the workings of the atmosphere.

Drought is caused by more than just a higher rate of evaporation compared to precipitation. As we saw in chapter 2, the real reason droughts happen is because the weather pattern shifts and carries moisture-bearing storm systems away from a region for an extended period of time. This allows evaporation to go to work on the land, as sunshine and wind dry things out. In the summer, these kinds of dry weather patterns are often accompanied by a heat wave, which worsens the situation.

So even though there may be more water vapor in the atmosphere, there are no weather systems around that can transform the water vapor into rainstorms. The extra humidity just hangs in the air, or gets blown by winds to another part of the country where the weather pattern is more active. There it may condense into rain-bearing clouds. In fact, it's common to see one part of the country

A drought, such as the one that led to this dust storm in western Texas, can occur when weather patterns shift storm systems and their moisture away from certain areas.

suffering under drought while another part of the country is drenched by above-average precipitation.

These regional differences in weather, from wet in one area to dry in another, apply to the earth as a whole. While droughts and wet spells come and go in many parts of the world, other parts of

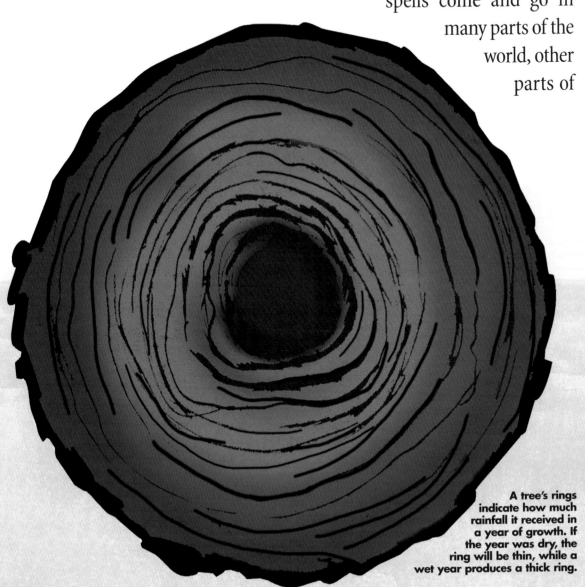

A tree's rings indicate how much rainfall it received in a year of growth. If the year was dry, the ring will be thin, while a wet year produces a thick ring.

the world are typically dry all the time or wet all the time. The Sahara Desert and the Amazon rain forest are examples of these types of climate extremes. In the future, therefore, drought will threaten some parts of the world more than others. The regions that are most likely to suffer from a drier climate are those that are already relatively dry. These regions are known as "semiarid."

Examples of semiarid regions include the Great Plains of the United States and the sub-Saharan region of Africa. The relatively dry climate in these parts of the world generally supports a landscape of grassland. Since these regions already get so little rain, perhaps ten to twenty inches per year, it would take only a nudge to make them more like a desert. The Sand Hills in Nebraska illustrate the kind of changes that occur when semiarid regions dry out.

Climatologists have also found evidence that severe and long-lasting droughts, of the kind that occurred in the 1930s, occur naturally every once in a while. They're not as extraordinary as we might think. Strong evidence for this comes from tree rings. Cutting into a tree shows how a tree grows, as each year of the tree's life is marked by a new ring of wood. If the year was dry, the tree ring will be thin. A wet year produces thick rings. One 1998 study on historical droughts documented tree ring records from California, Arizona, New Mexico, Nebraska, and Arkansas. They showed that a particularly devastating drought occurred across the western half of the United States in the last part of the sixteenth century. Researchers called this drought a "megadrought" because it was so dry and lasted for so long—nearly twenty years.

According to the scientists who authored the study, droughts of this kind could recur in the future. Data indicates that dust bowl–type droughts occur once or twice per century, on average. And a megadrought, lasting decades, occurs perhaps once every 500 years. Since the last drought of this kind occurred over 400 years ago, the chances of it occurring again in the next hundred years are not all that remote. Such a future megadrought would be devastating, with an economic cost enormous enough to rank it as one of the worst natural disasters to ever occur. The cause of a future megadrought would not necessarily be linked with global warming. However, global warming makes the possibility even more real.

Decades from now, in the last half of the twenty-first century, if the planet has warmed according to scientists' predictions, the average temperature of the earth may be several degrees Fahrenheit higher than it is today. Regionally, while some locations would remain as cool as today, others could heat up even more than the global average. The Great Plains of the United States may be one such area. A severe drought in the Plains states would have many effects.

Drought would damage the environment. Plants and animals would die, leading to a breakdown of the ecosystem. Higher temperatures would lead to an increased threat from wildfires. Dust storms might blow across the landscape once again in places that haven't seen them since the 1930s. This would contribute to the erosion of soil and even the desertification of some parts of the

Global warming could lead to severe droughts in areas such as the Great Plains, which could lead to soil erosion, dust storms, agricultural devastation, water shortages, and rationing.

Great Plains. Would the Nebraska Sand Hills awaken from their 1,500-year slumber?

The primary consequence for humans would be a lack of water. Researchers estimate that the average American uses over 100 gallons of water per day in the home. If global warming dries out the climate of the Plains states, water rationing may become a permanent necessity. Watering lawns, taking showers, running the dishwasher, flushing the toilet—these kinds of everyday activities could come under tight restrictions.

Agriculture would be one of the first victims of a water shortage in a future drought. Across the entire United States, crop irrigation

Aside from the Arkansas River in western Kansas, the only water source for irrigation in that part of the state is the Ogallala Aquifer, which is being drained faster than it is being replenished.

uses an estimated 140 billion gallons of water per day. This water comes from rivers, reservoirs, and wells that extract water from underground. In the Plains, the primary source of water is an underground reservoir known as the Ogallala Aquifer.

Stretching from South Dakota to western Texas, the Ogallala Aquifer covers well over 200,000 square miles of land. The problem is that water is being drawn from the Ogallala at an alarming rate. By one estimate, 60 percent of the aquifer's capacity has already been used. As farmers pump more water out of the aquifer, water levels drop. According to the United States Geological Survey, underground water levels have fallen fifteen to thirty meters across the central and southern Plains. The amount of farmland supplied by the Ogallala dropped by 20 percent in less than one decade in the 1970s and 1980s. And unlike many other underground reservoirs, the Ogallala is not quickly replenished by rainwater soaking through the ground. Experts fear that the rate of water withdrawal from the Ogallala will continue to outpace the rate of replenishment. Global warming would only worsen this water crisis.

The Great Plains, therefore, is a part of the world that teeters on the brink of drought. A severe drought, of the dust bowl variety, is by no means a certain event in our future. But it is a significant threat, one that looms larger if global warming proceeds as many scientists think. The dust bowl days are not necessarily a past event, confined to black-and-white photographs in history books. The Great Plains drought in the 1930s changed the way agriculture was practiced in the United States. A future drought, intensified by global warming, could do the same.

Conclusion

The global warming trend observed in the last part of the twentieth century raises critical questions for our future. Scientists think that the planetary warming is largely caused by the increasing amounts of greenhouse gases in the atmosphere from the burning of fossil fuels. If the warming trend continues, the earth's climate may undergo a change unlike any seen in thousands of years.

Skeptics remain. They point to uncertainties in the tools that scientists use to predict future climate. These computerized climate models are good at forecasting trends and large-scale patterns, but they do a poor job at simulating the vast inner-workings of the atmosphere. Since the climate models leave out many of the details, some scientists wonder how reliable they are.

Still, one of the results that most climate models predict is an energized hydrologic cycle. The rate at which water is pumped up and down between the air and the land, through condensation and evaporation, may increase as temperatures rise in the future. A consequence of this change could very well be an increase in the severity and length of droughts.

Worldwide, the supply of water is critical. Global population may rise as high as nine billion by 2050. A rising population means an increasing need for water. There are many regions of the world where the climate is already dry, and water is already scarce. Combine rising population with rising temperatures and more severe, long-lasting regional droughts, and the potential increases for famine and conflict as people compete for the dwindling supply of water and food.

History has shown how important the supply of water is, not only for plants and animals, but for people and civilizations. Droughts have been among the most destructive of all natural disasters. They strike slowly, almost invisibly, stealing water from the earth. At their worst, they can cause famine that can kill thousands. Droughts are one of the most important consequences that may arise from global warming and a changing climate.

Glossary

blocking pattern A weather pattern
in which a large area of high
air pressure blocks rain-bearing
storm systems from moving
across a region for a long period
of time.

climate The average weather conditions over a long period of time,
generally decades or more.

climate model A computerized
simulation of the atmosphere,
used by scientists to predict
changes in climate over long
periods of time.

condensation   The process whereby invisible, gaseous water vapor changes into liquid water.

desertification   A change in landscape from grassland to desert, sometimes caused by severe drought.

dust bowl   The most severe drought of the twentieth century in the United States, occurring in the 1930s in the Plains states.

El Niño   A warming of ocean water to above-average levels in the tropical eastern Pacific Ocean.

evaporation   The process whereby liquid water changes into invisible, gaseous water vapor.

evapotranspiration   The name given to the combined processes of evaporation and transpiration, in which water evaporates into the air from the surface of the earth and from plants.

fossil fuel   Any fuel made from the decayed remains of ancient plant and animal life; includes coal, natural gas, and oil. Fossil fuels take millions of years to develop.

global warming   The warming of the planet due to increasing amounts of greenhouse gases in the atmosphere.

greenhouse effect   The natural warming effect that the atmosphere has on the earth; arises from the exchange of radiation between the air and the ground.

greenhouse gas   Any gas that efficiently absorbs outgoing radiation from the earth. The main greenhouse gases are water vapor, carbon dioxide, methane, nitrous oxide, chlorofluorocarbons (CFCs), and ozone.

humidity   A measure of the amount of water vapor in the air.

hydrologic cycle   The transfer of water in gaseous, liquid, and solid form between the atmosphere, the earth, and the oceans.

ice core   A long tube of ice drilled out of an ice sheet or glacier. Scientists examine trapped air bubbles from thousands of years ago to get an idea of the earth's climate.

La Niña   A cooling of ocean water to below-average levels in the tropical eastern Pacific Ocean.

precipitation   Snow, rain, or anything else that forms inside a cloud and falls to the ground.

radiation   Energy in the form of invisible electromagnetic waves that travel at the speed of light.

runoff   The gravity-driven flow of water on land from high elevation to low elevation and eventually into the oceans.

transpiration   The process by which plants release some of their stored water into the air through pores on the undersides of their leaves.

water vapor   The invisible, gaseous form of water.

For More Information

Environmental Protection Agency (EPA)
Ariel Rios Building
1200 Pennsylvania Avenue NW
Washington, DC 20460-0003
(202) 260-2090
Web site: http://www.epa.gov/
    globalwarming
The EPA's global warming Web site is a good source for general information on our changing climate.

National Climatic Data Center (NCDC)
Federal Building
151 Patton Avenue

Asheville, NC 28801-5001
(828) 271-4800
Web site: http://www.ncdc.noaa.gov
The NCDC Web site contains information on precipitation records and major drought events of the last twenty years.

National Drought Mitigation Center
236 L.W. Chase Hall
P.O. Box 830749
University of Nebraska-Lincoln
Lincoln, NE 68583-0749
(402) 472-6707
Web site: http://enso.unl.edu/ndmc/index.html

Weatherwise Magazine
Heldref Publications
1319 18th Street NW
Washington, DC 20036-1802
(202) 271-6267
Web site: http://www.weatherwise.org
A popular magazine about all things weather.

For Further Reading

Allaby, Michael. *Droughts* (Dangerous Weather Series). New York: Facts on File, 1997.

—. *Water: Its Global Nature.* New York: Facts on File, 1992.

Bender, Lionel. *Heat and Drought.* Chatham, NJ: Raintree/Steck-Vaughn, 1998.

Farris, John. *The Dust Bowl.* San Diego: Lucent Books, 1989.

Newson, Lesley. *Devastation! The World's Worst Natural Disasters.* New York: Dorling Kindersley, 1998.

Ocko, Stephanie. *Water: Almost Enough for Everyone.* New York: Atheneum, 1995.

Steinbeck, John. *The Grapes of Wrath*. New York: Penguin
    Books, 1999.
Stevens, William K. *The Change in the Weather: People,
    Weather, and the Science of Climate*. New York:
    Delacorte Press, 1999.

Index

About the Author

Paul Stein has a B.S. in meteorology from Pennsylvania State University. He has eight years' experience as a weather forecaster, most recently as a senior meteorologist for the Weather Channel. Currently, he develops computer systems and software that display and process weather-related data.

Photo Credits

Cover image © Photo Researchers, Inc.: drought.
Cover inset © NASA/JPL/NIMA: topographic image of Bahia state, Brazil.
Front matter and back matter © Weatherstock: drought in western Texas.
Introduction background © Corbis: Great Salt Lake Desert, Utah.
Chapter 1 background © Weatherstock: ice storm in southeast Arizona.
Chapter 2 background © Corbis: parched earth.
Chapter 3 background © AP/Worldwide: Texas during a drought.
Chapter 4 background © Weatherstock: desert in southeast Arizona.
P. 7 © FSA/AP/Worldwide; pp. 12, 14, 16, 25, 36, 42, 49 © Corbis; p. 20 © Mankato Free Press/AP/Worldwide; p. 21 © National Park Service/AP/Worldwide; p. 22–23 © TOPEX/Poseidon, NASA, JPL; pp. 26, 30, 50 © AP/Worldwide; pp. 31, 45 © Weatherstock; p. 33 © David Crisp and the WFPC2 Science Team (Jet Propulsion Laboratory/California Institute of Technology); p. 34 © National Science Foundation/AP/Worldwide; pp. 38–39 © MODIS Land Science Team; p. 46 © Thomas Forget.

Series Design and Layout

Geri Giordano